TABLE OF CONTENTS

CHAPTER 1
Prophecy: I Am Demonstrating the Power of a Decree

"I decree and declare..." These are four words we hear prayer warriors cry out in the heat of the battle—but often without an experiential revelation of the power of a prophetic decree.

In 2019, God will begin demonstrating the power of a decree with rapid breakthrough following. Holy Spirit is pouring out revelation on Job 22:28 to believers who can believe Christ's delegated authority positions us as more than priests who petition and wait on the Lord in faith, sometimes for years. Christ's delegated

authority also positions us as kings who decree and see an immediate response in the natural realm.

Certainly, the power of a decree is nothing new. It's an ancient principle for establishing law in the spirit realm that even secular kings and rulers translate to the natural realm. However, as a times and seasons prophet I sense a strong wind of the Spirit on rhema and prophetic decrees in this hour of history. Rhema decrees are decrees from the Word of God that He is revealing to your spirit as a "now" strategy. Prophetic decrees are decrees that emanate from your anointed mouth through a Holy Spirit-inspired utterance.

Building Faith for Prophetic Decrees

I've been teaching and preaching on decrees for years. In fact, it was one of the strategies I emphasized in my best-selling book *Waging Prophetic Warfare*. But we have stepped into a season where this strategy will prove especially effective among those who gain revelation into the tremendous power that backs decrees. I heard the Lord say:

"Far too many of My people are begging Me to do what I've already promised I would do. Far too many are making supplication, bargaining with Me to do My revealed will, petitioning and crying out from a place of hope instead of faith.

"But I am calling My body to rise and decree what I have already said, to prophesy what I've already said, to declare what I've already said and to see My will and My Kingdom established in the earth.

"There is a time for every purpose under heaven. There's a time to pray the prayer of faith. There's a time to war with a prophetic word. There's a time to make supplication. There's a time to release the prayer of consecration. But in this season, I am demonstrating the power of a decree released by the leading of My Spirit through a heart of faith. Decree a thing and it shall be established."

Indeed, Job 22:28 (KJV) assures us, "Thou shalt also decree a thing, and it shall be established unto thee: and the light shall shine upon thy ways."

Different translations shed interesting light on this verse. For example, the NIV tells us, "What you decide on will be done, and light will shine on your ways." The Contemporary English Version puts it this way: "He will do whatever you ask, and life will be bright."

The AMPC version expounds on this truth a little more: "You shall also decide and decree a thing, and it shall be established for you; and the light [of God's favor] shall shine upon your ways." And The Message Translation assures, "You'll decide what you want and it will happen; your life will be bathed in light."

If you embrace this prophetic word—and by embrace I don't mean just saying "yes and amen" but put your faith on it and working it out by walking it out and speaking it out—you'll see radical change in your life. You'll see God open the windows of heaven, reconcile relationships, heal your body and more.

Moving From Hope to Faith
Many will say "amen" to this prophecy without walking in its truth, so I am

8

compelled to go deeper with the teaching in this book. These pages are dedicated to teaching you how to embrace the reality of your identity as a king and release God-pleasing decrees that bring results. But first, I want to comment on some aspects of this prophecy so the enemy doesn't enter in with confusion.

Holy Spirit said: "Far too many of My people are begging Me to do what I've already promised I would do. Far too many are making supplication, bargaining with Me to do My revealed will, petitioning and crying out from a place of hope instead of faith."

We'll deal more with this aspect as we move deeper into the teaching. For now, I want to point you to James 5:16: "The effective, fervent prayer of a righteous man accomplishes much."

James pointed out that effectual or effective prayer produces results. That means some prayer can be ineffective. If we pray ineffective prayers, we're not going to see answers.

What is effective prayer? It's the right prayer for the situation. Just as a golfer would

use a specific club for a specific shot or a surgeon a specific instrument for a specific surgery, you need to pray the right kind of prayer.

Begging and bargaining is not what God is looking for. He delights in the prayers of the righteous (see Proverbs 15:8). Begging and bargaining are for the hopeful. Decrees and declarations are for those who have faith according to Numbers 23:19-20:

"God is not a man, that He should lie, nor a son of man, that He should repent. Has He spoken, and will He not do it? Or has He spoken, and will He not make it good? See, I have received a commandment to bless, and He has blessed, and I cannot reverse it."

Re-Decreeing and Re-Prophesying
Next, Holy Spirit said: "But I am calling My body to rise up and decree what I have already said, to prophesy what I've already said, to declare what I've already said and to see My will and My Kingdom established in the earth."

While so many believers are rushing toward the next revelation, there is so power

in this one that we need to dwell on it—
meditate upon it. Although I believe in the
reality of present-day truth, I also believe
there is nothing new under the sun (see
Ecclesiastes 1:9). In other words, God's truth
is timeless and eternal. He doesn't invent new
truth as He goes along, but reveals or
highlights truth previously hidden at strategic
times. Much the same, He re-emphasizes
truth presently forgotten at strategic times.

God is saying in this prophecy we
need to decree what has already been said.
What He has said can be found, in part, in His
Word. God's Word is His will. He has
revealed His will about many issues of life in
His Word and left record of it so we can re-
decree a thing and see it established or, in
some cases where the enemy has meddled, re-
established. We can also re-decree what the
Holy Spirit has revealed as His will over our
lives, families, cities and nations.

Likewise, we can re-prophesy
prophetic utterances in Scripture as the Holy
Ghost leads us. We see a prime example of
this in Acts 2:17, where Peter re-prophesies
Joel's Old Testament prophecy: "In the last

11

days it shall be,' says God, 'that I will pour out My Spirit on all flesh; your sons and your daughters shall prophesy, your young men shall see visions, and your old men shall dream dreams."

Over and again, we see Old Testament prophecies repeated in the New Testament, establishing a pattern for re-prophesying in a kairos time. Here are just a few to prove the point:

Isaiah 40:3, "The voice of him who cries out, 'Prepare the way of the Lord in the wilderness, make straight in the desert a highway for our God. Let every valley be lifted up, and every mountain and hill be made low, and let the rough ground become a plain, and the rough places a plain; then the glory of the Lord shall be revealed, and all flesh shall see it together, for the mouth of the Lord has spoken it."

This prophecy spoke of John the Baptist. John declared this prophecy over himself in Luke 3:4-6, "As it is written in the book of the words of Isaiah the prophet, saying: 'The voice of one crying in the wilderness: 'Prepare the way of the Lord;

make His paths straight. Every valley shall be filled and every mountain and hill shall be brought low; and the crooked shall be made straight and the rough ways shall be made smooth; and all flesh shall see the salvation of God.'"

Isaiah 11:1-2 prophecies of the coming Christ: "And there shall come forth a shoot from the stump of Jesse, and a Branch shall grow out of his roots. The Spirit of the Lord shall rest upon him, the Spirit of wisdom and understanding, the Spirit of counsel and might, the Spirit of knowledge and of the fear of the Lord."

In Luke 4:16-21, Jesus declares this prophecy over Himself: "He came to Nazareth, where He had been brought up. And as His custom was, He went to the synagogue on the Sabbath day. And He stood up to read. The scroll of the prophet Isaiah was handed to Him. When He had unrolled the scroll, He found the place where it was written:

'The Spirit of the Lord is upon Me, because He has anointed Me to preach the gospel to the poor; He has sent Me to heal the

broken-hearted, to preach deliverance to the captives and recovery of sight to the blind, to set at liberty those who are oppressed; to preach the acceptable year of the Lord.'

Then He rolled up the scroll, and He gave it back to the attendant, and sat down. The eyes of all those who were in the synagogue were fixed on Him. And He began to say to them, 'Today this Scripture is fulfilled in your hearing.'"

Malachi 4:5-6 assures: "See, I will send you Elijah the prophet before the coming of the great and dreaded day of the Lord. He will turn the hearts of the fathers to their children, and the hearts of the children to their fathers, lest I come and strike the earth with a curse."

Jesus re-prophesied in Luke 1:15-17: "For he will be great in the sight of the Lord, and shall drink neither wine nor strong drink, and he will be filled with the Holy Spirit, even from his mother's womb. He will turn many of the sons of Israel to the Lord their God. And he will go before Him in the spirit and power of Elijah, to turn the hearts of the fathers to the children and the disobedient to

the wisdom of the just, to make ready a people prepared for the Lord."

Understanding the Times and Seasons
In the prophecy, the Lord said: "There is a time for every purpose under heaven. There's a time to pray the prayer of faith. There's a time to war with a prophetic word. There's a time to make supplication. There's a time to release the prayer of consecration. But in this season, I am demonstrating the power of a decree released by the leading of My Spirit through a heart of faith. Decree a thing and it shall be established."

God establishes the concept of times and seasons in Ecclesiastes 3:1-8. Although this is not meant to be an exhaustive list, it demonstrates the way of God:

"To everything there is a season, a time for every purpose under heaven: a time to be born, and a time to die; a time to plant, and a time to uproot what is planted; a time to kill, and a time to heal; a time to break down, and a time to build up; a time to weep, and a time to laugh; a time to mourn, and a time to dance; a time to cast away stones, and a time

to gather stones; a time to embrace, and a time to refrain from embracing; a time to gain, and a time to lose; a time to keep, and a time to cast away; a time to tear, and a time to sew; a time to keep silence, and a time to speak; a time to love, and a time to hate; a time of war, and a time of peace."

We're in a season of the decree. Those with a sons of Issachar anointing are hearing God's wisdom and revelation in this hour: 1 Chronicles 12:32 describes them as "those having understanding of times and what Israel should do."

We're in a Job 22:28 season. Job 22:28 (KJV) assures us, "Thou shalt also decree a thing, and it shall be established unto thee: and the light shall shine upon thy ways."

CHAPTER 2
What the Bible Says About Decrees

D ecree. The word has lost some of its power in our modern world. A quick scan of news headlines reveals this watering down. Decrees of divorce are easy to get. Fiscal decrees are readily appealed in governments. Some police officers around the country violate decrees at will. Technology companies breach federal decrees.

A decree is "an order usually having the force of law," according to *Merriam-Webster*'s dictionary. But it seems decrees don't always carry the weight in the natural realm they should. Make no mistake, though, decrees do carry weight in the spirit realm.

According to *Baker's Evangelical Dictionary of Biblical Theology*, "Decrees issued by rulers, written commands having the effect

of law, and the metaphor of God as King of the world provide the imagery behind the Bible's references to God's 'decrees.'"

Decrees are common in judicial systems around the world. But the genesis of this concept is rooted in God. Think about it for a minute. God decreed the world into existence. I'll say that again: God decreed the world into existence.

You've probably heard God spoke the world into existence. But what He spoke was a clear decree. You've heard it said that God spoke, "Let there be light" (Genesis 1:3). That's an unfortunate translation. A more accurate translation of what God actually said was "Light be." He decreed light into existence.

God framed the world with His decree. Hebrews 11:3 tells us, "By faith we understand that the universe was framed by the word of God, so that things that are seen were not made out of things which are visible." He decreed what was not seen and it manifested, according to His will. We can operate in decrees in the same way, according to His will.

God's Decrees Are Law

Decrees are not a willy-nilly statements made nonchalantly or in passing. Decrees carry weight. Beyond creation, God Himself has made certain decrees—decrees that cannot be changed. The prophet Moses decreed them as law (see Deuteronomy 33:4). While Scripture doesn't always use the word decree, the concept it is implied in that God established commandments as Kingdom laws. The prophets and apostles of the Bible have outlined this reality. Here are three Scriptures that demonstrate this point:

Isaiah 14:26-27 reveals: "This is the purpose that is purposed on the whole earth, and this is the hand that is stretched out on all the nations. For the Lord of Hosts has purposed, and who shall disannul it? And His hand is stretched out, and who shall turn it back?"

Isaiah 46:9-10, "Remember the former things of old, for I am God, and there is no other; I am God, and there is no one like Me, declaring the end from the beginning, and from ancient times the things that are not yet

done, saying, 'My counsel shall stand, and I will do all My good pleasure...'"

Ephesians 1:11, "In Him also we have received an inheritance, being predestined according to the purpose of Him who works all things according to the counsel of His own will..."

Again turning to *Baker's Evangelical Dictionary of Biblical Theology* we read: "In Exodus 7-14 God shows his decrees to be sovereign over Pharaoh's by 'hardening' Pharaoh's heart. This 'hardening' involves the creation of an irrational mind-set. Despite the miraculous plagues, Pharaoh refuses to do the reasonable thing (decreeing Israel's release from bondage), thereby bringing further disaster on himself and his land. In the early stages of the story Pharaoh appears to be a free agent, hardening his own heart (Exodus 8:15) but as the story develops God is increasingly portrayed as the direct cause of Pharaoh's stupidity. Pharaoh is ultimately reduced to a mere puppet of Yahweh (Exodus 14:4; Exodus 14:8).

God takes decrees seriously. Leviticus 18:4 reminds, "You shall follow My decrees

and keep My ordinances to walk in them: I am the Lord your God." God issues the exact same warning in Leviticus 18:26, Leviticus 20:22, Leviticus 25:18.

When the Israelites defied His decrees, trouble followed. 2 Kings 7:15 paint a clear picture: "They rejected His statutes and His covenant that He had made with their fathers and the decrees He had given them. They followed idols, and became idolaters, and followed the surrounding nations, concerning whom the Lord commanded them, that they should not do like them."

The ABCs of Decrees

We can decree the Word of God or the revealed will of God through prophecy. There is power in the Word of God. Heaven and earth will pass away, but His Word will never pass away (see Matthew 24:35). His Word is life to all those who find them and healing to the flesh (see Proverbs 4:22). His Word will add length to your life and give you peace (see Proverbs 3:1). The grass withers and the flowers fade away but the Word of God will stand forever (see Isaiah 40:8). His Word is

spirit and life (John 6:63). His Word is truth (see John 17:17). His Word is pure, like silver tried in a furnace, purified seven times (Psalm 12:6).

Hebrews 4:11-16 explains: "Let us labor therefore to enter that rest, lest anyone fall by the same pattern of unbelief. For the word of God is alive, and active, and sharper than any two-edged sword, piercing even to the division of soul and spirit, of joints and marrow, and able to judge the thoughts and intents of the heart. There is no creature that is not revealed in His sight, for all things are bare and exposed to the eyes of Him to whom we must give account.

"Since then we have a great High Priest who has passed into the heavens, Jesus the Son of God, let us hold firmly to our confession. For we do not have a High Priest who cannot sympathize with our weaknesses, but One who was in every sense tempted like we are, yet without sin. Let us then come with confidence to the throne of grace, that we may obtain mercy and find grace to help in time of need."

God expects us to follow His decrees (Leviticus 18:4). The enemy is also bound to obey a prophetic declaration in the name of Jesus, the name at which every knee must bow and every tongue confess that He is Lord (see Romans 14:11).

You Shall Decree a Thing

We're in a Job 22:28 season. Job 22:28 (KJV) assures us, "Thou shalt also decree a thing, and it shall be established unto thee: and the light shall shine upon thy ways."

Different translations shed interesting light on this verse. For example, the NIV tells us, "What you decide on will be done, and light will shine on your ways." The Contemporary English Version puts it this way: "He will do whatever you ask, and life will be bright." The AMPC translation says: "You shall also decide and decree a thing, and it shall be established for you; and the light [of God's favor] shall shine upon your ways." And The Message puts it this way: "You'll pray to him and he'll listen; he'll help you do what you've promised. You'll decide what you

want and it will happen; your life will be bathed in light."

Pulpit Commentary sheds some light on this Scripture: "Thou shalt also decree a thing, and it shall be established unto thee. Whatever thou resolvest on, i.e., God shall ratify with his authority, and bring to pass in due time for thy benefit - a promise which has certainly "a touch of audacity" about it (Cook). David is less bold, but intends to give the same sort of encouragement when he says, 'Delight thyself in the Lord, and he shall give thee the desires of thine heart; commit thy way unto the Lord; trust also in him; and he shall bring it to pass' (Psalm 37:4-5)."

We can decree like God, as long as we're decreeing His will. We can decree the decrees of God, the Word of God, and what the Holy Spirit leads us to decree prophetically. Abraham and Joshua are two figures in the Bible who walked in this revelation. They weren't ordained as kings in Israel. Israel at that time did not have kings. But they understood this aspect of their rights and responsibilities as leaders.

Abraham issued decrees over his life. He has a covenant with God, just like you do. He had a specific promise from God, just like you do. He issued decrees, just like you can. A decree is more than a positive confession. Remember, a decree carries the force of law. Romans 4:17 (AMPC) tells us, "As it is written, I have made you the father of many nations. [He was appointed our father] in the sight of God in Whom he believed, Who gives life to the dead and speaks of the nonexistent things that [He has foretold and promised] as if they [already] existed."

When Joshua found himself in a war because he vowed to make intercession for the Gibeonites, he decreed: "Sun, stand still over Gibeon; and moon, in the Valley of Aijalon." So the sun stood still, and the moon stood in place until the people brought vengeance on their enemies. Is this not written in the book of Jashar? The sun stood still in the middle of the sky and did not set for about a full day. There has not been a day like this either before or after it, when the Lord obeyed a man, for the Lord waged war for Israel (Joshua 10:12-14).

Joshua didn't beg God to make the sun stand still and the moon stand in its place. Joshua didn't petition God. Joshua understood his authority and he issued a decree. God backed it up.

CHAPTER 3
Your Royal Priesthood

Believers have a duality of standing in the role of both kings and priests. Most believers are comfortable with the priestly anointing but have not embraced the kingly anointing. The concept of priest has been etched in many believers' minds.

From a world's perspective—and even from a Hebraic perspective—the role of king and priest are entirely different. These offices represent two distinct functions. A priest did not rule and a king did not offer sacrifices.

The Old Testament makes a clear distinction between the two in 1 Samuel 13. King Saul led the Israelites into war against

the Philistines. When the enemy gathered to launch a counter strike against Saul's battalion, Saul was intimidated by the number of warriors, which the Bible describes as "like the sand which is on the seashore" (see 1 Samuel 13:5). 1 Samuel 13:6-12 tells the rest of the story, including Saul's unlawful priestly demonstration:

"When Israel's fighting men saw that they were in a strait (for the people were distressed), then the people hid themselves in caves, in hollows, among rocks, and in cellars and cisterns. Some of the Hebrews went over Jordan to the land of Gad and Gilead.

"But as for Saul, he was still in Gilgal, and all the people followed him, trembling. He waited seven days, according to the set time that Samuel had appointed. But Samuel did not come to Gilgal, and the people were scattered from him. Saul said, 'Bring here to me the burnt offering and the peace offerings.' Then he offered the burnt offering. When he finished offering the burnt offering, Samuel came. And Saul went out to meet him to greet him.

"Samuel said, 'What have you done?'

"And Saul said, 'Because I saw that the people were scattered from me, and that you did not come to the appointed assembly days, and the Philistines are gathering themselves together at Mikmash, therefore I said, 'The Philistines will come down now upon me to Gilgal, and I have not yet appeased the face of the Lord.' So I forced myself, and offered the burnt offering."

"Samuel said to Saul, 'You have done foolishly. You have not kept the commandment of the Lord your God, which He commanded you. Truly now, the Lord would have established your kingdom over Israel forever. But now your kingdom will not continue. The Lord has sought for Himself a man after His own heart and the Lord has commanded him to be prince over His people, because you have not kept that which the Lord commanded you."

Samuel was a priest. Saul was a king. It was out of God's order for him to perform the priestly function. Priest come from the line of Levi. Samuel was a Benjamite. Just as there was a difference between the priest and king in the Old Testament, there is a

difference between priest and king today. The difference is, in Christ, believers can operate in both functions. The key to victory in prayer is to operate in the right anointing at the right time.

Our Perpetual Priestly Anointing

We see the rise of the priesthood in the Old Testament. Melchizedek was the first priest mentioned in the Bible (see Genesis 14:18). Interestingly, Melchizedek was both a king and a priest, and many theologians argue he was a pre-incarnate appearance of Christ. Hebrews 7:17 calls Jesus "a priest forever, in the order of Melchizedek."

After Melchizedek, we see the Levitical priesthood, which offers more insight into the priestly anointing. The priest's duties were many, but centered primarily on serving as a representative of the people before God, offering sacrifices and performing rituals.

Priests also are seen using the Urmin and Thummin, which helped them determine the will of God. Priests blessed the people (see Numbers 5:22-27), as well as oversaw

purification rituals (see Numbers 19), collected tithes, maintained the temple, blew the trumpet during feasts, taught the people and offered counsel.

As you can see, these are spiritual functions rather than governmental functions. Priests have authority over the matters of God's house and God's people. Kings have authority over the matter of realms and regions.

We still see the priestly anointing in the New Testament. We know there was a change in the priesthood (see Hebrews 7:12). All believers are considered priests serving under the leadership of the High Priest, who is Jesus. Jesus was not a Levite. He was from the tribe of Judah (see Hebrews 7:14). We're not Levites. We're in Christ. So the priesthood looks different in the New Testament.

In Romans 15:15-16, Paul wrote: "Nevertheless, brothers, I have written even more boldly to you on some points, to remind you, because of the grace that is given to me from God, that I might be a minister of Jesus Christ to the Gentiles, in the priestly service

ιe gospel of God, so that the offering of Gentiles might be acceptable, being sanctified by the Holy Spirit."

Jesus Christ is now our great High Priest. Hebrews 4:15 tells us: "Since then we have a great High Priest who has passed into the heavens, Jesus the Son of God, let us hold firmly to our confession. For we do not have a High Priest who cannot sympathize with our weaknesses, but One who was in every sense tempted like we are, yet without sin."

We can discern our role as priests in the New Testament by understanding how Jesus operates in the priestly ministry. Hebrews 7:25 tells us "He at all times lives to make intercession" for us and Romans 8:34 tells us He is "at the right hand of God and is also interceding for us."

Although Christ still performs other functions—1 John 2:1-2 reveals He is our advocate when we sin; John 14:1-3 tells us He is preparing a place for us in Heaven; and we know He is building His church and ruling as its head—His main role as High Priest is to make intercession.

We are in Christ. We are seated with Him in heavenly places at the right hand of the Father (see Ephesians 2:6). As priests, we are seated in a place of intercession. We may perform other priestly functions, such as taking up offerings or ministering in the house of the Lord. But in the realm of prayer, we're lifting up needs to the Father in the name of Jesus from a priestly position.

Most intercessions stand in the role of priest. Governmental intercessors must shift into the role of a king.

CHAPTER 4
Embracing Your Kingship

Jesus is the King of kings and the Lord of lords (see Revelation 19:16). Have you ever wondered who these kings are? Is the Bible speaking of David, Nebuchadnezzar, Solomon, Saul, Cyrus and other kings we read about in Scripture? Yes and no.

Although Jesus is the King and ruler of all, Revelation 19:16 speaks of more than His dominion but also kings who are called to stand in His delegated authority. Those kings are believers who are seated with Him in heavenly places (see Ephesians 2:6). In other words, we are the kings.

This can be hard for many believers to believe because we've been taught to stand as priests

in our home, prophets in the marketplace and intercessors who petition the Lord in the name of Jesus. However, Scripture makes this duality absolutely clear over and over again.

Revelation 1:6 says He has made us "kings and priests to His God and Father."

Romans 5:17, "For if by one man's trespass death reigned through him, then how much more will those who receive abundance of grace and the gift of righteousness reign in life through the One, Jesus Christ."

1 Peter 2:9, "But you are a chosen race, a royal priesthood, a holy nation, a people for God's own possession, so that you may declare the goodness of Him who has called you out of darkness into His marvelous light."

Revelation 2:6, "Blessed and holy is he who takes part in the first resurrection. Over these the second death has no power, but they shall be priests of God and of Christ and shall reign with Him a thousand years."

Revelation 5:9-10, "And they sang a new song, saying: 'You are worthy to take the scroll, and to open its seals; for You were slain, and have redeemed us to God by Your

blood out of every tribe and tongue and people and nation, and have made us kings and priests unto our God; and we shall reign on the earth."

What Kings Do

With a clear understanding of what priests do, we can explore what kings do and readily discern clear distinctions. You'll see a stark contrast in the functions that will help you understand why it's important to pray from the right position and authority.

Kings have a domain

As of the time of this writing, there are 26 monarchs in the world, including kings and queens, sultans, emirs and emperors who rule and reign in 43 nations of the world. Kings have a domain in which they exercise authority.

Paul understood the concept of a domain. In 2 Corinthians 10:13 (AMPC), he writes, "We, on the other hand, will not boast beyond our legitimate province and proper limit, but will keep within the limits [of our commission which] God has allotted us as our

measuring line and which reaches and includes even you."

The word "limit" in that verse is the Greek word "metron." According to *Strong's Concordance*, it means a "measure, portion measured off, determined extent, or limit." Kingdoms have boundaries around a domain. This is the place they can rightly exercise their authority. The boundaries within which we work is the Word of God. If the Word says it, we have authority to enforce it. We can enforce Christ's healing power, His promise of provision and other decrees of God.

We also have measure of authority in particular domains. Let me illustrate this point. I was in London in 2017 ministering. During the break, I was having lunch with prophet who lives in Windsor, making her essentially a neighbor to the Queen of England who lives in Windsor Castle.

After lunch, she said, "The queen will receive a prophetic word from you."

I said, "The queen?"

"Yes."

"You mean *the* queen?"

There are so many Christians who call themselves Queen or Princess these days, I just had to be certain she wasn't speaking of someone on her staff.

"Yes," she said.

"You mean the Queen of England? Queen Elizabeth?"

"And when will she receive this word?"

"In 15 minutes. I'll leave you to pray."

Needless to say, I went to praying in the Holy Ghost! The Lord gave me a word for the queen and it was delivered to her. I respect the Queen of England. My heritage is largely British, according to my DNA test results. I honor the queen. She is a fine

Christian woman who sends a gospel message to her nation every Christmas.

Most people in the world respect Queen Elizabeth. A recent news report called her "The world's queen." But the reality is she does not have any dominion beyond the United Kingdom. When she visits America, she has no authority. She cannot change our laws. She cannot decree a thing and see it established.

Likewise, although you have authority to stand on the Word of God in any area of your life, you rule and reign as a king in certain metrons. Your authority to rule and reign is typically relegated to a certain mountain. I am speaking of the seven mountains of influence.

Loren Cunningham, founder of Youth With a Mission, and the late Bill Bright, founder of Campus Crusade for Christ (now called CRU), received the same revelation from the Lord in 1975: In order to revolutionize the world for Jesus, the church needs to wield influence in the seven mountains of society—religion, family,

education, government, media, arts and entertainment, and business.

God gave mankind dominion over the earth in Genesis 1:26: "Then God said, 'Let us make man in our image, after our likeness, and let them have dominion over the fish of the sea, and over the birds of the air, and over the livestock, and over all the earth, and over every creeping thing that creeps on the earth.'"

Of course, we know Adam committed high treason. Later Jesus took dominion back from the devil and gave His followers a mandate to rule and reign with Him (see 2 Timothy 2:12). We will rule and reign in greater measure in eternity but there is a rulership in this age. Jesus said, "Occupy until I come" (Luke 19:13). That Greek word occupy is "pragmateuomai." *The KJV New Testament Greek Lexicon* translates it as: "to be occupied in anything; to carry on a business."

As Jesus was about His Father's business, we must be occupied with our Father's business in the sphere of influence to which He has called us (see Luke 4:29). We are charged with walking worthy of the

vocation to which we are called (see Ephesians 4:1). As ministers of reconciliation and ambassadors of Christ (see 2 Corinthians 5:18-20), we may have a natural occupation but we also have a spiritual vocation. And we are warned not to hide our light under a bushel (see Matthew 5:15).

Entire books have been written on the seven mountains of society. Beyond Bright and Cunningham, men of God like Francis Schaeffer, Bob Buford, Os Hillman, Ed Silvoso and Lance Wallnau have worked to forward this revelation. We don't have time in this short book to explore all the facets of this theology, but we will look briefly at each of the seven mountains.

Every believer has been given a sphere of influence and authority in one of these mountains. Exploring each mountain individually will help you clearly identify, with the leading of the Holy Spirit, the mountain to which you are called. The following definitions are attributed to Generals International's Reformation Prayer Network, whose primary goal is to be a catalyst through prayer and righteous activism to bring change

to these areas of societal influence. You can find more about the network at www.generals.org/rpn. You can also join my prayer movement at awakeningblaze.com.

The Mountain of Religion

Every society has some type of belief in a superior being or beings. In the east, religions tend to be polytheistic (many gods) or outright idolatrous (such as Hinduism and Buddhism). Although these religions are thousands of years old, they nonetheless continue to thrive today. In the west, Christianity and Catholicism are predominant, but postmodern views are increasingly being accepted and the concept of God is being rejected. This is especially true in Europe.

The Christian Church is described in the Greek language as the ecclesia. Literally translated, the word ecclesia means "governing body." Although we don't condone theocracies, this translation suggests that the Church should have great influence in all other spheres that make up a society. With a plethora of categorized religions around the world, it's the Church's responsibility to reach

the lost with the love and Gospel of Jesus Christ, and expand the Kingdom in ministerial efforts, both nationally and internationally.

The Mountain of Family

In any functional society, the family is the "building block" of the community. Throughout the Bible, you will find familial examples that portray how we ought to live our lives today. God desires that men, women, and children within a family be united as one in His love. After all, He is the ultimate Father (Romans 8:14-17).

The families of the United States have been under constant and prolonged attack. Today, the assailants are fatherlessness, divorce (50% rate in secular and Christian marriages), abuse, homosexual marriage, pornography, and other negative influences have brought great dysfunction to American life. God is calling fathers and mothers (both spiritual and biological) to bring order to the chaos that the enemy has unleashed against families in America. He also wants to bring healing to marriages and relationships within families in order to maintain a moral

foundation for children in the future to stand upon.

The Mountain of Education
At one time the education system of America unapologetically incorporated the Bible, prayer to the God of the Bible, and biblical values in every aspect of school life. Not coincidentally, this system produced a people that produced the most powerful and prosperous nation the earth has ever seen.

Now, the children of our nation are inundated with liberal ideologies, atheistic teaching and postmodern principles in our public schools and in most universities (including many Christian institutions). Put simply; they are being indoctrinated with often false, biased and anti-biblical information. A re-introduction of biblical truth and Bible-centric values is the key to renewal and restoration in America's failing education system.

The Mountain of Government
Proverbs 14:34 states that, "righteousness exalts a nation, but sin is a reproach to any

people." Many times, as exemplified in the Old Testament, a nation's moral standards are dependent on those exhibited by its leaders (or predominant political party). While each individual is responsible for his or her own sins; the fact remains that people are greatly influenced by those moral (or lack thereof) that popular leaders adopt.

The progressive liberal agenda, empowered by well-known men and women in the arts and entertainment industries, have made significant gains in the political arena over the past few decades. In fact, many liberal groups, such as the ACLU, seek to remove anything related to God or Christianity from the governmental and educational systems because of a misapplied interpretation of the phrase, "separation of church and state." We must see a shift in this arena in order to preserve the Christian heritage that America was founded upon. The goal is to put in place righteous political leaders that will positively affect all aspects of government.

The Mountain of Media

The media mountain includes news sources such as radio, TV news stations, newspapers, Internet news and opinion (blog) sites and etc. The media has the potential to sway popular opinion on current issues based upon its reporting, which is not always truthful or accurate. In the 2008 elections, the liberal "elite" media played a vital role, especially in the Presidential race. Their generally supportive and positive reporting greatly influenced the outcome.

There has been a rise in Christian news services, which is needed. However, to bring transformation to the mountain of media, Christians who are gifted for and called into this type of work must be willing to report righteously and truthfully in the secular marketplace.

The Mountain of Arts & Entertainment

In this mountain we find some of the most influential forces shaping our society. Music, filmmaking, television, social media, and the performing arts drive the cultural tastes,

values and standards of a nation's citizens, particularly its youth.

With a heavy reliance on the strong appeal of sex, drugs and alcohol, the arts and entertainment industries wield significant influence. The body of Christ needs powerful, righteous men and women who are not afraid to take their God-given talent into the arts and entertainment arenas. People ready to further His purposes, while impacting those who are lost in darkness and would not otherwise be interested in any kind of Christian message in traditional forms.

The Mountain of Business

The ability to literally create wealth through ingenuity, enterprise, creativity and effort and is a God-given gift and a universal impulse. The markets and economic systems that emerge whenever people are free to pursue buying and selling become the lifeblood of a nation. This includes anything from farms to small businesses to large corporations.

Of course this realm is prone to corruption through idolatry, greed and covetousness. In response, the Church must

embrace its responsibility to train up ⸺
who are called into the marketplace to m⸺
businesses and provide leadership ⸺
integrity and honesty. We believe it is the
Lord's will to make his people prosperous and
that He desires for His Church to use its
wealth to finance the work of Kingdom
expansion. Simply put: Prosperity with a
purpose.

Pray this prayer with me: *Father, in the
name of Jesus, help me to identify the mountain I am
to conquer for Your glory. Like Caleb and Joshua as
they spied out the Promised Land, help me see myself
as well able to take the land. Give me a "different
spirit" as they had so I will charge ahead in your grace
to accomplish Your will in the mountain of influence
in which you've called me to operate."*

Kings have authority to govern
Even in the secular world, there is a political
doctrine that espouses the divine right of
kings. This doctrine states kings derive their
authority from God and could not therefore
could not therefore be held accountable for
their actions by any earthly authority such as a
parliament, according to *Encyclopedia Britannica*.

The natural monarch's power was said to run equivalent to the award of spiritual power to the church.

Kings have authority to govern. Govern means "to control and direct the making and administration of policy" and "to control, direct, or strongly influence the actions and conduct of" and "to exert a determining or guiding influence in or over, according to *Merriam-Webster*'s dictionary.

1 Timothy 2:2 speaks of praying for "kings and all those in authority." So, we see there are natural kings and spiritual kings that carry different spheres and measures of authority. As a king under the lordship of Christ the King, Jesus secured your authority. You have authority to preach the gospel and to stand against the works of darkness. Jesus told His disciples, "Look, I give you authority to trample on serpents and scorpions, and over all the power of the enemy. And nothing shall by any means hurt you" (Luke 10:19).

Kings have power
Kings have power. How much? Take Queen Elizabeth II as an example. As the ruler of the

kingdom, she signs off on proposed bills before they become laws. She can grant a royal pardon to anyone convicted of a crime. She appoints advisors and cabinet officials, issues passports, commands the armed forces, declares war and could even dissolve the parliament.

As a king under the kingship of Jesus Christ, we also have power. As a king, you have the power to declare war on the enemy. You have power to force out evil spirits (see Matthew 10:1). The power that raised Christ from the dead dwells in you (see Romans 8:11). You have power to enforce God's will in the earth.

Kings have influence
Kings have influence. Influence is the power of capacity of causing an effect in indirect or intangible ways, the act or power of producing an effect without apparent exertion of force or direct exercise of command, and an emanation of spiritual or moral force. Jesus, the King of kings, has influenced countless millions to believe the gospel through His words, His signs, His wonders, His miracles

and His believers (his kings) who share His message and do the greater works (see John 14:12). The teachings of Christ have also influenced writers, philosophers, and even other religions, for thousands of years. As a king, you have influence if you let your light shine.

Kings are warriors
Kings are warriors. The Bible shows us time and time again kings going to war, from Saul to David to Ahab to Jehoshaphat and beyond. Kings are warriors. Paul tells his spiritual son Timothy to be a good soldier (2 Timothy 2:3) and to war a good warfare (1 Timothy 1:18). Paul told us succinctly that "we wrestle not against flesh and blood, but against principalities, against powers, against the rulers of the darkness of this world, against spiritual wickedness in high places" (Ephesians 6:12). As kings, you war for God's will in your life and in the lives of others.

Kings judge with wisdom
In the Bible, we see kings judging. King Solomon judged between two women who

had a dispute over a baby. The each had infants but when one of them died, each claimed the living baby was her own. King Solomon used wisdom to judge between the two, flushing out the true mother and returning the child to its proper care. (You can read this account in 1 Kings 3).

Kings conquer and occupy territories
Roman emperors conquered much of the known world in their day. But they didn't just conquer the territory, they occupied it and influenced its culture. Likewise, Alexander the Great, king of Macedonia and Persia, is remembered as one of the early world's most brilliant minds.

According to History.com, "By the time he died 13 years later, Alexander had built an empire that stretched from Greece all the way to India. That brief but thorough empire-building campaign changed the world: It spread Greek ideas and culture from the Eastern Mediterranean to Asia. Historians call this era the "Hellenistic period." (The word "Hellenistic" comes from the word Hellazein, which means "to speak Greek or identify with

the Greeks.") It lasted from the death of Alexander in 323 B.C. until 31 B.C., when Roman troops conquered the last of the territories that the Macedonian king had once ruled."

Jesus said and occupy until He comes (see Luke 19:13). We are to be salt and light, both these elements influence their surroundings. As kings, we are to conquer hearts for Christ, conquer lands, and make disciples of nations (see Matthew 28:18-20).

Matthew Henry's Commentary tells us, "Christ must reign till all enemies be put under his feet. The reason of the victory is, that he is the King of kings, and Lord of lords. He has supreme dominion and power over all things; all the powers of earth and hell are subject to his control. His followers are called to this warfare, are fitted for it, and will be faithful in it."

Kings decree
In the earlier chapter, I gave you example after examples of how kings issue decrees

CHAPTER 5
Discerning When to Stand as a King

There's a time to operate in your priestly anointing. There's a time to operating in your kingly anointing. The key is to determine the right time for the right action.

As the Preacher said: "To everything there is a season, a time for every purpose under heaven: a time to be born, and a time to die; a time to plant, and a time to uproot what is planted; a time to kill, and a time to heal; a time to break down, and a time to build up; a time to weep, and a time to laugh; a time to mourn, and a time to dance; a time to cast away stones, and a time to gather stones; a

time to embrace, and a time to refrain from embracing; a time to gain, and a time to lose; a time to keep, and a time to cast away; a time to tear, and a time to sew; a time to keep silence, and a time to speak; a time to love, and a time to hate; a time of war, and a time of peace" (Ecclesiastes 3:1-8).

Solomon didn't go so far as to say there's a time to pray like a priest and time to pray like a king, but the "every purpose under heaven" portion of this Scripture covers it. Again, don't get me wrong. I'm not advocating that we neglect our biblical role as priests. I'm suggesting, rather, that you discern the times and seasons in the realm of intercession. I'm exhorting you to understand spiritual dynamics.

I run into Christians all the time who have been praying for a single promise of God—from healing, to deliverance, to breakthrough in some other area, and do not see the promise come to pass. Of course, it could be that these believers are praying amiss according to James 4:3. It could also be the enemy is delaying their promise. But could it be possible that these precious believers are

praying from the wrong stance? Could it be possible that they need to stop petitioning and start decreeing?

Many Christians seem to beg God. I hear them pray this way, "Lord, if you'll just do this one thing for me, I'll never ask you to do anything for me again." If they don't make it to that extreme, often they pray weak prayers hoping rather than believing. A king doesn't hope his decree will come to pass. He knows it's a done deal as soon as the decree is issued.

Beloved, we don't need to beg God to do what He has already promised to do—or, moreover, to do what He's already accomplished in Scripture through salvation. We don't need to beg Him to pay our bills or heal our bodies. Psalm 37:25-26 assures us, "I have been young, and now am old; yet I have not seen the righteous forsaken, nor their offspring begging bread. The righteous are gracious and lend, and their offspring are a source of blessing."

We don't need to beg God. We are not His charity cases; we are His children. We don't need to sit by the gate beautiful asking

alms like the beggar Peter and John healed. We need to receive what He has done for us. We need to decree His Word because His Word is His will and you can safely decree His will in the earth with full confidence that He is watching over His Word to perform it (see Jeremiah 1:12).

The Holy Spirit showed me something magnificent in my study on decrees. This revelation relates to the prayer bowls in heaven. Intercessors love to talk about the prayer bowl. We find this concept in Scripture: "When He had taken the scroll, the four living creatures and the twenty-four elders fell down before the Lamb, each one having a harp, and golden bowls full of incense, which are the prayers of saints" (Revelation 5:8).

In his book, *The Amazing Discernment of Women*, Jentezen Franklin offers some insight into these bowls that's worth repeating:

"What a marvelous image! When you pray, you are filling the prayer bowls of heaven. In God's perfect timing, your prayers are mixed with the fire of God (His power) and cast back down to earth to change your

situation Your prayers don't just bounce off the ceiling; they rise like incense before the throne of God. Even if you don't feel like anything is happening in the natural world, when you pray, you are filling the prayer bowls in the spirit realm. When they are full, they will tilt and pour out answers to your prayers!"

I agree. We are filling the bowls with our prayers. But I also believe our decrees can tip the bowl over. I believe we need to pray as a priest, but I believe there comes a tipping point in the prayer bowl; a time when our intercession has set the stage for an overflow. The petitions and intercessions set the stage for the overflow. Many times, it takes a different strategy to break all the way through—to see the wobbling bowls tip all the way over and pour out a blessing from the windows of heaven we cannot contain. I believe that strategy is the decree.

Again, you don't decree as a priest. You decree as a king. In building our faith for the kingly decree, it's worth looking at king's decrees in the Bible. In the next section are

some passages the Holy Spirit led me to highlight.

King's Decrees Are Irrevocable

Ezra 5:13, "However, in the first year of Cyrus the king of Babylon, King Cyrus made a decree to rebuild this house of God." A king's decree is irreversible. King Darius understood this. When he heard about Cyrus' decree, he was obligated to search it out. We see this playout in through the Book of Ezra:

"Then Darius the king issued a decree and a search was made in the house of records, where the treasures were stored in Babylon. At Ecbatana, in the provincial palace of the Medes, a scroll was found, and in it the following record was written: 'In the first year of Cyrus the king, the same Cyrus the king issued a decree concerning the temple of God at Jerusalem" (Ezra 6:1-3).

Again, a king's decree is irreversible. In the book of Daniel, King Darius made a decree that anyone who worshipped any other god would be thrown into the lion's den. In Daniel 6:10-12, we read:

"Now when Daniel learned that the decree had been published, he went home to his upstairs room where the windows opened toward Jerusalem. Three times a day he got down on his knees and prayed, giving thanks to his God, just as he had done before. Then these men went as a group and found Daniel praying and asking God for help. So they went to the king and spoke to him about his royal decree: 'Did you not publish a decree that during the next thirty days anyone who prays to any god or human being except to you, Your Majesty, would be thrown into the lions' den?' The king answered, 'The decree stands—in accordance with the law of the Medes and Persians, which cannot be repealed.'"

King Darius did not want to throw Daniel into the lion's den. Daniel was his most trusted adviser. But the king had no choice. Into the lion's den Daniel went. The only way to supersede a king's decree is by issuing another decree. In the Book of Esther, King Ahasuerus made a decree that enabled the destruction of the Jews. This decree was irrevocable. But he issued a decree later that

the Jews could rise up and defend themselves (see Esther 8).

What are you decreeing over your life? If you've been issuing destructive decrees over your life with the words of your mouth, it's time to issue a new decree.

CHAPTER 6
Decrees Release Judgment Against the Enemy

Decrees release divine judgment against the enemy and his plans for your life. You may have made mistakes. You may even have fallen into sin. But when we repent we can decree Romans 8:28 over our life: "We know that all things work together for good to those who love God, to those who are called according to His purpose."

Hard to believe? Consider this: Even in the midst of God's judgement on the Israelites, He released these words to the prophet Jeremiah: "For I know the thoughts

and plans that I have for you, says the Lord, thoughts *and* plans for welfare *and* peace and not for evil, to give you hope in your final outcome" (Jeremiah 29:11, AMPC).

Along those same lines, Jesus told His disciples, "The thief comes only in order to steal and kill and destroy. I came that they may have *and* enjoy life, and have it in abundance (to the full, till it overflows)" (John 10:10). When the enemy tries to come in like a flood, your decree will lift up a standard of truth against him, often through your decree (see Isaiah 59:19).

The enemy's plans for you are evil. God's plans for you are good. As the late healing evangelist Oral Roberts used to say, "God is a good God. The devil is a bad devil." When evil comes into your life through the work of the wicked one, a decree can release God's judgement and restore your future and hope. I am a living example.

About 18 months after my husband disappeared and left our lives in a shambles, I was arrested for a crime I didn't commit. I was facing five years in prison—a sentence that would have left my daughter essentially

orphaned. The judge would not allow me out on bail, even with an ankle bracelet, even on home arrest, even though I didn't have any prior record and there was nothing but my word against another's. I was facing a minimum sentence of five years. My attorney suggested I take the plea to avoid getting a greater penalty.

Helpless and hopeless, I finally cried out to God—and He delivered me from the enemy's plot to destroy our lives. Wearing a bright orange jumpsuit in a dark county jail, I surrendered my heart to the One who created me, and the peace of God that passes all understanding guarded my heart and mind in Christ Jesus (see Philippians 4:7).

It was in this setting—a county jail filled with prostitutes, drug addicts, thieves, and all manner of violent criminals—that I heard the still, small voice of God for the first time. In this place of captivity, I discovered that where the Spirit of the Lord is, there is liberty (see 2 Corinthians 3:17). In the face of impossibility, God taught me that all things are possible to Him who believes (see Mark 9:23).

I'll never forget my experience. The Holy Spirit showed me in Word and spoke to my heart that I would be released in 40 days. Being a new convert, I had no idea that the number 40 was a symbol of testing and trial, but every time I opened my Bible, I read an account that revolved around that number: Moses's forty years in Egypt, the Israelites' forty years in the desert, Noah's experience with the forty-day flood, Jesus's forty days in the wilderness.

After several days of supernatural guidance through the Word, the Holy Spirit made it clear to my heart that I would be released from the injustice of imprisonment in 40 days. It seemed impossible, considering that the judge had refused to allow me bail three times—and that this same judge was on vacation well after the fortieth day of my captivity. It was impossible, really.

Nevertheless, I started decreeing the word of the Lord. I decreed to everyone who would listen that I was getting out on the 40th day. I didn't understand what I was doing, but I was decreeing freedom and declaring judgment on the enemy every single time I

said, "I'm going to be out on the fortieth day."

I told my bunkies (those who slept near me in the jail) I would be out on the fortieth day. I told the corrections officers I would be out on the fortieth day. I told my mother I would be out on the fortieth day. I said it over and over again, even though no one believed it. I decreed God's will over my life and brought judgment against the enemy's plans, which was to put me away for five years.

All I can say is, "But God." On the fortieth day, I was called into a holding cell with other inmates. One by one, they were taken before their accuser and judge. One by one, they came back, some celebrating a release and others crying because they were heading to prison for a long, long time. Eventually, I was left all alone, praying. That's when a bailiff came in and said my attorney was on the phone line in another room. I picked up the phone and my attorney asked, "Are you ready to go home?"

It was the fortieth day. Yes, that was about right. I was never tried or convicted by

my accusers. I never stood before an earthly judge. Thankfully, the Judge—Jesus Christ—is not a man that He should lie. I was released on the fortieth day, just as the Holy Spirit told me I would be. I decreed my way out of false accusations and into justice. I agreed with God and let His declaration over my life become my declaration and I saw judgment fall on the enemy as the judge ruled my incarceration a gross error of injustice.

CHAPTER 7
Decrees Establish the
Will of the Lord

Window Rock, Arizona. It's a small city—and the governmental capital of the Navajo Nation. The Navajo Nation is the largest territory of a sovereign Native American Nation in North America. It's called Window Rock because the major landmark in the city is a massive rock with a hole through the middle, like a window.

But Window Rock is more than a famous landmark—it's also one of four places where the Navajo medicine men carry their woven water jugs to gather water for a ceremony during which they ask false gods for rain. Indeed, Window Rock is a site marked by the medicine men's witchcraft. A local told

me there were demons stationed around the famed rock and anyone who got too close came under fierce attack.

Of course, I didn't know that last part when we set out to do a prophetic act at the rock-with-the-hole-through-it. See, the Navajo Nation has serious water supply issues. According to the non-profit DigDeep, if you are born Navajo, you're 67 more times likely not to have a tap or toilet in your house than other Americans.

On top of that, the suicide rate among Native American adults grew 65.2 percent from 1990 to 2010, according to the Centers for Disease Control. The Department of Justice reveals Native Americans are 2.5 times more likely to be sexually assaulted than other Americans. Poverty, unemployment, low graduation rates, debilitating diseases, cardiovascular disease obesity and alcoholism plague the Navajo Nation.

The medicine men don't seem to be curing anything that ails the Navajo Nation with its witchcraft. That's why our apostolic team decided to obey the Holy Spirit and break the curse of the nation. We headed out

to Window Rock and a small group from our team bee-lined for the rock-with-the-hole-through-it. The only problem is there was a chain-linked fence in between us and the epicenter.

When I failed to squeeze through the five-inch opening between the fence and rock, two of the apostles hoisted me over the wall with a prayer cloth and clear instructions to break curses and release healing. So there I stood, one small spec against a massive orange rock background, standing in the gap for a nation in crisis, crying out to the Lord to break in with light, and blessing a people who have lived under a curse for hundreds of years. I tucked the anointed prayer cloth tightly in the cleft of a rock and made my way back over the fence, surprisingly, without ripping my jeans.

Within three months, we started seeing the early fruit of this prophetic act. The Navajo Nation launched a nationwide search for a police chief after being without one for several years. Navajo Nation schools received $45 million in federal funding that was held up for 12 years. Wholesome Wave and the

Navajo Nation have partnered to increase access to healthy foods. A Navajo judge was convicted of abusing his office by showing favor to defendants—members of his family—in a burglary investigation. The Navajo Nation closed its first-ever bond transaction, selling nearly $53 million of investment-grade tax-exempt bonds to fund infrastructure projects. And the list goes on.

We are not presuming to say that this one prophetic act set all of these blessings in motion. We were one of many groups how visit the Navajo Nation, which is home to many strong churches that pray without ceasing. But we do believe we played a part in pushing back some of the darkness that's invading the lives of these precious people. The job is not done. More intercession is needed. More warfare needs to be waged. But this one prophetic act combined with a decree contributed some color to the bigger picture.

CHAPTER 8
Decrees Shift Circumstances

Decrees shift circumstances. God Himself declares, "For as the rain comes down, and the snow from heaven, and do not return there but water the earth and make it bring forth and bud that it may give seed to the sower and bread to the eater, so shall My word be that goes forth from My mouth; it shall not return to Me void, but it shall accomplish that which I please, and it shall prosper in the thing for which I sent it" (Isaiah 55:10-11).

I had to remember that when our church building partially collapsed in August 2018 while I was hosting an intercessory

prayer retreat in Kansas City. We were driving in the rain when a text came in from one of our members at Awakening House of Prayer (AHOP). Tracey wrote in to tell us AHOP was all over the news.

"Awesome," I joked with our staff. "It's about time the community recognizes our good works."

Apparently, we were in the news because of the back wall of our building collapsing. We were displaced. All our property was locked in the building, including $100,000 of media, worship and office equipment. We didn't know where to go or what to do. Thankfully, a local museum opened up his meeting room for the first Sunday and we were able to find hotel space in the interim.

As I was sitting in my prayer chair asking the Lord what was going on. It was a Job 1 season and there had been one attack after another after another after another. The building was the grand finale of the enemy's destructive work. Suddenly, the Lord reminded me of a prophetic word Chuck Pierce, an apostle and prophet and president

of Glory of Zion Ministries in Texas, released when he was ministering at our church about nine months earlier.

The prophecy was about a shaking at AHOP. Chuck prophesied the walls would shake, the roof would shake, and God was going to shake us out of that place. Of course, we all thought it was a spiritual shaking. But it was a natural shaking. As it turns out, a construction crew was doing ground work just feet from the building and the vibrations apparently caused the back wall to crumble. Chuck prophesied AHOP would be known as the house that shook. And so it was... AHOP was all over the news.

God reminded me of that prophecy and told me, "It's good you have so many intercessors praying over this issue. But you need to get up and take charge." See, there are times when kings send soldiers into battle and there are times when the king leads them into battle. The Lord was charging me with leading this battle. I got up and began to make decrees for two hours. Suddenly, something came out of my mouth that shocked me.

"I decree on or before 8/18/18 we will have papers for our new building, in the name of Jesus." I was stunned. We had been stuck in a 2,000-square-foot box for six and a half years. We had searched high and low for an affordable, suitable facility. We had been wandering around in the wilderness. We couldn't find anything anywhere, largely due to zoning. It seems in South Florida zoning officials would rather approve condos and retail than churches.

I was glad nobody heard my decree because it was incredulous. How would we have papers on a new building in two days? I wasn't going to tell anyone, but the Lord told me to keep decreeing it.

I asked the Lord, "How am I supposed to find this building, Lord?

He said, "Go look on Craigslist."

"Craigslist?"

There was silence. I obeyed. I found a listing within 15 minutes that was perfect for our church. I had one of my staff call in. Unfortunately, it was already secured for a charter school but the broker said they were having trouble getting the permit. Do you know why? Because that was my building. On 8-18-18, we had a letter of intent signed for the new building and the landlord approved it. Our old building had one six-by-six-foot office we all shared, no children's facility, and two bathrooms. Our new facility is 10,000 square feet with a room for the infants, children, youth, TV studio, classrooms, security room, several offices and 13 bathrooms, as well as a green room and storage areas. The decree shifted an impossible circumstance, brought AHOP out of the wilderness and into its promised land.

CHAPTER 9
Decrees Activate Angels

Biblical scholars can argue whether angelic activity is increasing in this hour, but prophetic voices insist angels are on assignment with increasing intensity. As heirs of salvation, we must understand the many functions of angels and cooperate with the Lord and His angels to see His good, perfect and acceptable will come to pass in our lives.

Speaking of angels, the Bible says, "Are they not all ministering spirits sent out to minister to those who will inherit salvation?" (Hebrews 1:14) From this verse we see the apostolic nature of angels—God sends them on ministry assignments to help

us. God ultimately chooses if and when to send angels, but we can release activation prayers that set the stage for God to respond with angels.

Psalm 103:20 reveals how angels work with decrees: "Praise the LORD, you his angels, you mighty ones who do his bidding, who obey his word. Praise the LORD, all his heavenly hosts, you his servants who do his will."

When our church facility collapsed, leaving us displaced, one my spiritual sons called me—moments after I made the 8/18/18 decree. He had no idea that I had been praying and decreeing for hours or what I had released. That's what made his vision so powerful. He shared that he saw a contract being signed and angels delivering that contract. I agreed and decreed and within two days we had the contract.

Angelic Activity Is Rising

Tim Sheets, author of *Angel Armies*, says angelic activity will now increase dramatically. He has seen an increase of angelic activity in his own life, and has completed a

comprehensive study of angels over the past decade.

"Angels assist Holy Spirit and the heirs of salvation (Hebrews 1:14) to do God's will upon the earth. They work to enforce the decrees of God's Word (Psalm 103:20). We are living in the season of the greatest move of God in history. Angels are needed to help facilitate that move," Sheets says.

"Also, the Word of God is now being released in faith decrees as never before. Millions of them. This is activating angels to assist Holy Spirit to bring them to pass. In 2007 as Holy Spirit began to download a revelation concerning angel armies. He spoke this to me, 'The greatest days in church history are not in your past, they are in your present and your future.' To see those days increased angel activity is a must."

Biblical scholars can argue whether angelic activity is increasing in this hour, but prophetic voices insist angels are on assignment with increasing intensity. As heirs of salvation, we must understand the many functions of angels and cooperate with the

Lord and His angels to see His good, perfect and acceptable will come to pass in our lives.

Speaking of angels, the Bible says, "Are they not all ministering spirits sent out to minister to those who will inherit salvation?" (Hebrews 1:14) From this verse we see the apostolic nature of angels—God sends them on ministry assignments to help us. God ultimately chooses if and when to send angels, but we can release activation prayers that set the stage for God to respond with angels.

In the realm of angelic revelation, we must take caution to remain balanced. 1 Peter 5:8 (AMPC) offers a clear warning: "Be well balanced (temperate, sober of mind), be vigilant and cautious at all times; for that enemy of yours, the devil, roams around like a lion roaring in fierce hunger], seeking someone to seize upon and devour."

Just as there are many believers who reject the notion that an angel can appear with a message, assist in healing ministry, or execute some other assignment for the Lord, there are others who put too much emphasis on angels and still others who make up

encounters with strangely-named angels that don't exist.

Jesus Is Superior to Angels

We must remember Jesus is superior to the angels. The writer of Hebrews rightly pointed out in Hebrews 1:5-13:

"For to which of the angels did He at any time say: 'You are My Son; today I have become Your Father'? Or again, 'I will be a Father to Him, and He shall be a Son to Me'? And again, when He brings the firstborn into the world, He says 'Let all the angels of God worship Him.'

"Of the angels He says: 'He makes His angels spirits, and His servants a flame of fire.' But to the Son He says: 'Your throne, O God, lasts forever and ever; a scepter of righteousness is the scepter of Your kingdom. You have loved righteousness and hated wickedness; therefore God, Your God, has anointed You with the oil of gladness more than Your companions.'

"And, You, Lord, laid the foundation of the earth in the beginning, and the heavens are the works of Your hands. They will perish,

but You remain; and they all will wear out like a garment; as a cloak You will fold them up, and they will be changed.

"But You are the same, and Your years will not end.' But to which of the angels did He at any time say: 'Sit at My right hand, until I make Your enemies Your footstool'?"

Even—and especially—in the context of angel activations, it's vital we don't displace Father, Son and Holy Spirit in our lives. The Father sent Jesus to pay the price for our sins and pave the way to salvation. Jesus sent the Holy Spirit.

Jesus told His disciples: "But the [a]Helper (Comforter, Advocate, Intercessor—Counselor, Strengthener, Standby), the Holy Spirit, whom the Father will send in My name [in My place, to represent Me and act on My behalf], He will teach you all things. And He will help you remember everything that I have told you" (John 14:26, AMPs).

Jesus has the preeminence in our lives. He can choose to dispatch angels, but the choice is His. The Bible admonishes us to acknowledge God in all our ways and He will

direct our paths (see Proverbs 3:6). It doesn't say to acknowledge angels in all our ways. The Bible says to seek first the kingdom of God and His righteousness and everything we need will be added to us (see Matthew 6:33). It doesn't say to seek first angels.

There are different times and reasons and seasons to activate specific angels on assignment in your life. I believe the Holy Spirit gives us an unction or a leading to activate those angels by praying His Word and declaring His will. When we're sensitive to the Holy Spirit's voice, we will discern the unction to release angels to function.

As you move through the angel activations in the coming chapters, be careful not to give glory to angels that belongs only to God; be careful not to exalt angels to a place that belongs only to Jesus; and avoid relying on angels when you should be depending on the Holy Spirit.

Remember angels obey the Lord—not man: "Bless the Lord, you His angels, who are mighty, and do His commands, and obey the voice of His word" (Psalm 103:20).

Chapter 10
Decrees Unlock Provision

Decrees unlock provision. I've seen it in my life over and over—but especially in this season since the Lord dusted of the decree revelation.

In the book of Ezra, King Cyrus issued a royal decree to rebuild the temple at Jerusalem. (Ezra 5:13) That decree was backed up with royal resources—and the proclamation of that decree unlocked the generous giving and volunteering of those who heard it. (See Ezra 1.)

It started with a prophetic word Chuck Pierce spoke over my life. I was at Christian International with Bishop Bill Hamon. After the service, an usher tried to

escort me through a side door in the sanctuary but Bishop found me and took me a different route. That's when we bumped into Chuck, who said, "I'm glad I ran into you. I have a word for you." The prophecy revealed God would send me into 37 cities to raise up troops to throw Jezebel off a wall—and that God would pay for it.

Some months later, an international prophet sent me an e-mail asking me if I would go to four nations to teach at his School of the Prophets. My assignment: raise up troops to throw Jezebel off the wall. I thought, "That sounds like Chuck's word." The prophet told me he could not pay my way and I should pray about it. I prayed and decided it was the will of the Lord.

The first stop was Nigeria. Because of my schedule, I could only stay on the ground for one day. It was actually less than 24 hours. The flight was $5,000 and 36 hours both ways. That was 72 hours in the air and less than 24 hours on the ground with a $5,000 bill to boot. I discussed it with the Lord. That discussion went something like this:

"Lord, I don't think spending $5,000 on this trip is being a very good steward. I'll only be there for one day. And the Lord said, "It's not about how long you're there. It's about what you deposit while you're on the ground."

I needed $5,000. God gave me an idea to raise the money by starting a missions arm at JenniferLeClaire.org/missions. I raised $4,000 but with two days left before the trip, I still needed $1,000 more.

The Lord gave me a strategy: "Sow $1,000."

"No, Lord. You don't understand. I need $1,000."

"Sow $1,000," He repeated.

I obeyed. I sowed $1,000. But I was led in that moment not just to sow a thing but to decree a thing. I learned that when I sow and decree, there's opportunity for a rapid harvest. I only had two days to get the harvest. I am sure you can figure out what

happened: The $1,000 came in right on time. The trip was paid for.

But watch this. On my way out of Nigeria a woman gave me a plain white envelope. Inside were 10 fresh $100 American bills. When I got back home, there was a check in the mail for $5,000. I am convinced the decree unlocked this provision.

But that wasn't the end of the story. When I was walking through the AHOP building collapse situation, one of my spiritual sons, who is a seer, called me and said he saw in the spirit a woman struggling over writing my ministry a check for $10,000. The Lord spoke to her about writing it but it was such a large amount she was hesitating. Of course, we needed those funds at a time when the building collapse caused a major disruption in our ministry. I decreed that the Lord's will would be done over that donation.

A few days later, a check came in the mail. Only it wasn't for $10,000—it was for $25,000. I thought to myself, "Well, he saw a check but he needs bifocals. He got the amount wrong." But lo and behold, a few days later a check came in for $10,000. Guess

how much it cost to move into our newbuilding? That's right, about $35,000. Decree a thing—decree God's will—and it shall be established.

I hear many, especially spiritual warriors, commanding angels. I cannot find in Scripture anywhere we are to command angels. Psalm 91:1 (AMP) says, "For He will command His angels in regard to you, to protect and defend and guard you in all your ways [of obedience and service]." And "Bless the Lord, you His angels, who are mighty, and do His commands, and obey the voice of His word." Decrees activate angels.

CHAPTER 11
Decrees Release Favor

Decrees release favor. The Amplified Classic translation of Job 22:28 makes this plain: "You shall also decide *and* decree a thing, and it shall be established for you; and the light [of God's favor] shall shine upon your ways."

Through the many years I've known Mama Cindy Jacobs, I've only ever received one prophetic word from her. It was actually a spiritual observation and a decree. She said: "You are in a season of crazy favor." Ever since that moment, I have walked in extraordinary favor with God and man.

Favor is vital. We know Jesus grew in favor with God and man (see Luke 2:52). Noah found favor in God's eyes and it lead to deliverance for him and his household (Genesis 6:8). Both Joseph and Daniel found favor in the midst of captivity. Ruth found favor with Boaz. David found favor with Jonathan. Esther found favor with the king and saved the Jewish people.

Consider these reminders of His favor:

Psalm 5:12, "For You, Lord, will bless the righteous; You surround him with favor like a shield."

Psalm 90:17, "Let the beauty of the Lord our God be upon us, and establish the work of our hands among us; yes, establish the work of our hands."

Psalm 84:11, "For the Lord God is a sun and shield; the Lord will give favor and glory, for no good thing will He withhold from the one who walks uprightly."

Psalm 30:5, "For His anger endures but a moment, in His favor is life; weeping may endure for a night, but joy comes in the morning."

Psalm 89:17, "For You are the beauty of their strength; by Your favor our horn is exalted."

God's favor is God's grace. Decree God's favor over your life according to the promises of God. God's favor can touch every area of your life, from your mind to your body and from your relationships to your finances. God's favor can establish you in ways you have never imagined, open doors, close doors and empower you.

CHAPTER 12
Corporate Decrees Make the Devil Flee

C orporate decrees make the devil flee. You've heard about the concept of corporate prayer and corporate worship, but corporate decrees kick it up a notch.

You can build a flight team through corporate decrees. What is a flight team? We find this concept in Leviticus 26:8, "Five of you shall chase a hundred, and a hundred of you shall put ten thousand to flight; your enemies shall fall before you by the sword."

Deuteronomy 32:30 and Joshua 23:10. We first see this concept in Deuteronomy: "How should one chase a thousand, and two

put ten thousand to flight" and later we see another witness to its power in Joshua: "One man from among you can make a thousand flee, for it is the Lord your God who wages war for you, as He told you."

Of course, I've long understood the power of corporate decrees but a friend of mine shared with me her story of the flight team. She was facing an obstacle that she just could not seem to overcome on her own. As she was praying about this seemingly insurmountable mountain, the Lord gave her a strategy: Build a flight team. She was puzzled by this statement and inquired of the Lord what He meant exactly. That's when he pointed her to Deuteronomy 32:30.

The key to fruitful corporate decrees—or any decree for that matter—is found in Psalm 68:11-12, "The Lord gave the word; great was the company of women who proclaimed it: 'Kings of armies flee; they flee!'" Notice the key to this Scripture: the Lord gave the word and the people proclaimed, or decreed, it. But the lynchpin is unity. There is power in unity.

Corporate prayer and decrees unleash multiplied power of God. I believe this is because God loves unity. The Psalmist reveals where there is unity, God commands a blessing (see Psalm 133). Jesus Himself assures us: "Again I say to you, that if two of you agree on earth about anything they ask, it will be done for them by My Father who is in heaven. For where two or three are assembled in My name, there I am in their midst" (Matthew 18:19-20).

CHAPTER 13
Decrees Shift Spiritual Climates Atmospheres

D ecrees shift spiritual climates and atmospheres over our lives and even our cities and nations. Scientists will tell you that the earth's seasons have shifted in recent years—and they point to climate change as the foundation for the shift. What is a climate? According to *Merriam-Webster*, a climate is "the average course or condition of the weather at a place usually over a period of years as exhibited by temperature, wind velocity and precipitation."

If we translate this to spiritual realities, we learn that the spiritual climate over your life may take years to establish. For example, the enemy can't establish a climate of fear

over your life with one "boo." Much the same, the Holy Spirit can't establish a climate of intimacy over your life with one hour of fellowship every once in a while. By definition, developing a climate of any kind take time.

Natural climates manifest through temperature. It takes time for Christians to become lukewarm. It tends to happen little by little. It takes time for Christians to catch the fire of God and turn red hot. It may seem like these things happen overnight or in an instant, but the reality is both God and the enemy are at work in our lives. If we give the Holy Spirit permission, He will spark a fire in us that grows to a raging inferno of passion for Jesus. If give the devil access, he will quench our fire and passion for God.

Both these spiritual scenarios happen little by little until we reach a tipping point where we feel or discern the shift in our minds and hearts. In other words, we may not feel ourselves growing hungrier for God or losing our passion for Jesus until one day we're hot or cold. The good news is, even if you are cold God can set you on fire again.

You can change the spiritual climate over your life.

Natural climates are marked by wind velocity. Wind is one symbol for the Holy Spirit. Velocity is the speed at which something moves. When the devil's winds slam against your house, it brings drama, trauma and possible destruction—unless your house is built on Christ (see Matthew 7:27). When the Holy Spirit's wind blows, we see life emerge in situations that seem hopeless, refreshing come to the weary, the love of God manifest in our midst, and even signs, wonders, healing and miracles.

Natural climates are marked by precipitation. Precipitation is rain, sleet, snow, mist or hail. The enemy brings storms in our life, but God brings restoration in the face of barrenness and loss. The Bible speaks of the former rain and the latter rain (see Joel 2:23) in terms of refreshing where there have been dry or barren seasons. The outpouring on the day of Pentecost is part of the latter rain. When the Holy Spirit pours out rain, He's pouring out hope.

The Climate Over Your Life

If we again translate all this to a spiritual reality—as natural surroundings often correspond to spiritual conditions—it's clear that changing our spiritual climate sets the stage for a shift in spiritual seasons. We can't shift our seasons—God does that. But we can create a climate that invites Him to do the work in our hearts that prepares us for the next season—we can move from a season of oppressive warfare to a season of oppressive victory.

What is the spiritual climate over your life? If you are angry, ungrateful, complaining, angry, greedy, controlling, critical, impatient, indifferent, discouraged, jealous, frightened, frustrated, unforgiving, resentful, bitter, selfish, or something of the like, you're creating a spiritual climate over your life that repels the Holy Spirit. He loves you, yes, but your flesh is warring against His Spirit.

If, by contrast, you are thankful, peaceful, prayerful, joyful, generous, forgiving, loving, content, self-less, hopeful, faithful, inspired, worshipful, you are creating an atmosphere that attracts the presence of God.

And the presence of the Holy Spirit is the ultimate key to spiritual change and growth. Put another way, we need to cultivate the fruit of the Spirit in our lives and reject the works of the flesh. In doing so, we position our hearts for God to shift us into fruitful seasons of harvest.

In her book, *Shifting Atmospheres: A Strategy for Victorious Spiritual Warfare*—a book I wholeheartedly endorsed—Dawna DeSilva writes[1]:

"Some people believe that ungodly atmospheres are the same thing as demonic spirits. While I do believe demonic atmospheres are presided over by the demonic realm, I do not believe the atmospheres themselves are actual demons. Atmospheres, for me, are the prevailing spiritual realities created by man's partnership with the entities residing in the spiritual realm. As the messages these spiritual beings emit are agreed upon and partnered with, the resulting atmosphere expands. Therefore, I see atmospheres, both godly and ungodly, as cyclical partnerings between broadcasts from

the spirit realm and man's participation with them…"

What you decree over your life will shift your spiritual climate for better or worse. What you decree over your city can shift the atmosphere for better or worse. (You can read more about this in my book, *The Spiritual Warrior's Guide to Defeating Water Spirits*.)

CHAPTER 14
What Are You Decreeing Over Yourself?

The power of death and life are in the tongue (see Proverbs 18:21). What if we believed that? What if we *really* believed that? No doubt, it would revolutionize our lives.

If we really believed Proverbs 18:21, we'd stop complaining about being sick and start decreeing healing. We'd stop worrying about finances and start decreeing the power to create wealth to establish God's covenant in the earth (see Deuteronomy 8:18). We'd stop whining and start winning.

What are you decreeing over yourself? Death or life? Proverbs 16:24 tells us whoever keeps his mouth and his tongue keeps himself

out of trouble and Proverbs 13:3 promises us if we guard our mouth we preserve or life while if we open our mouth wide we invite ruin. Your words can justify you or condemn you (see Matthew 12:37).

Are you decreeing trouble, ruin and condemnation? Again, I ask you, are you decreeing death or life? I want to drive the reality of the power of your tongue home by offering you multiple translations of Proverbs 18:21. Meditate on these verses before you open your mouth to say anything else.

"The tongue has the power of life and death, and those who love it will eat its fruit" (NIV).

"Words can bring death or life! Talk too much, and you will eat everything you say" (CEV).

"What you say can preserve life or destroy it; so you must accept the consequences of your words" (GNT).

"The tongue has the power of life and death, and those who love to talk will have to eat their own words" (God's Word).

"Words kill, words give life; they're either poison or fruit--you choose" (MSG).

Decrees Can Determine Your Destiny

The wrong decree sealed the fate of a generation that died in the wilderness and propelled others into their Promised Land. In Numbers 13, the Lord told Moses to send men into the land of Canaan to spy explore. One chief from each tribe accepted the assignment to see what the land is, how many and how strong were the people, how they lived and so on. The men were gone for 40 days.

The declarations they offered when they returned made Bible history and serve as a lesson to us today. Numbers 13:26-27 tell us:

"And they returned and came to Moses and to Aaron and to all the assembly of the children of Israel, to the Wilderness of Paran, to Kadesh, and brought back word to them and to the entire assembly and showed them the fruit of the land. They reported to him and said, 'We came to the land where you sent us, and surely it flows with milk and honey, and this is the fruit of it.'"

In other words, God's promise was true. Jehovah had told them He would bring them into a land flowing with milk and honey (see Exodus 3:17). The spies confirmed that God had accurately described the land. This should have built their faith in God's veracity, so the declaration they collectively issued in Numbers 13:28-29 was surprising:

"However, the people are strong that dwell in the land, and the cities are fortified and very great, and also we saw the children of Anak there. The Amalekites dwell in the land of the Negev, and the Hittites, and the Jebusites, and the Amorites dwell in the mountains, and the Canaanites dwell by the sea and by the edge of the Jordan."

Caleb had a different decree: "Caleb silenced the people before Moses and said, 'Let us go up at once and possess it, for we are able to overcome it.'" (Numbers 13:30).

"But the men that went up with him said, 'We are not able to go up against the people because they are stronger than we.' They gave the children of Israel a bad report of the land which they had spied out, saying, 'The land through which we have gone as

spies is a land that devours its inhabitants, and all the people whom we saw in it are men of great stature. And there we saw the giants, the sons of Anak, which come from the giants, and in our eyes we were like grasshoppers, and so we were in their eyes.'"

Caleb and Joshua, who the Bible says were of a different spirit (see Numbers 14:24), made a faith decree. The other 10 Israelite chiefs made a fear decree. The people wept and cried because the power of the death decree pierced their unbelieving hearts. The children of Israel started wishing they had never left Egypt and that they had died in the wilderness. They set their hearts to return to the bondage of Pharaoh. They picked up stones to hurl at Caleb and Joshua, who had released the power of life.

James 3:3-10 (MSG) brings a strong conclusion to this section:

"A bit in the mouth of a horse controls the whole horse. A small rudder on a huge ship in the hands of a skilled captain sets a course in the face of the strongest winds. A word out of your mouth may seem of no account, but it can accomplish nearly

anything—or destroy it! It only takes a spark, remember, to set off a forest fire. A careless or wrongly placed word out of your mouth can do that. By our speech we can ruin the world, turn harmony to chaos, throw mud on a reputation, send the whole world up in smoke and go up in smoke with it, smoke right from the pit of hell. This is scary: You can tame a tiger, but you can't tame a tongue—it's never been done. The tongue runs wild, a wanton killer. With our tongues we bless God our Father; with the same tongues we curse the very men and women he made in his image. Curses and blessings out of the same mouth!"

Avoiding Extremes

In the midst of the Word of Faith Movement, some believers twisted Kenneth E. Hagin's teachings on confessions into a name it-claim-it-blab-it-grab-it gospel. That wasn't Hagin's intention, but it soured many believers on the notion of confessing the Word. This is tragic and I shudder to think believers would misappropriate the power of a prophetic decree in this same way. You can't manipulate

God with your decrees. You can't decree the lusts of your own heart and expect to get a harvest of righteousness. You can't abuse scriptural concepts and anticipate godly results. Decrees are biblical but they must be biblical. In other words, we decree the Word of God or we issue decrees as led by God's Spirit, which ever disagrees with His Word. When we decree the Word or release prophetic decrees, we are standing on solid ground and results are guaranteed because, again, God's Word does not return to Him void. It accomplishes what He sends it to do through you (scripture). Your carnal nature will decree what it wants, what the devil wants--anything but what God wants. Your spirit man will decree the will of the Lord.

CHAPTER 15
Breaking Evil Decrees

Have you ever received a threat from a false prophet? If you have, you may have felt similar to Nehemiah when he encountered false prophets with accusations as he was rebuilding the wall.

I got an email from a well-known false prophet. If I called his name you would know him. The email contained threats over an article we posted at awakeningmag.com. I ignored it.

This false prophet has been part of high-profile scandals. He's divorced. His dirty laundry has been aired in public courtrooms. He's leading so many people astray. He has zero credibility except among those he has deceived, and this group will defend him as if their life depended on it. Messengers from

this false prophet also contacted our ministry through Facebook with threats.

My attitude was like the apostles in Acts 4:29-30: "Now, Lord, look on their threats and grant that Your servants may speak Your word with great boldness, by stretching out Your hand to heal and that signs and wonders may be performed in the name of Your holy Son Jesus."

The email read threatened me with an FBI investigation and blackmail videos were prepared with false, edited footage that was largely focused on others issues but attached my name to it by association. Of course, the videos were full of lies, spliced videos, cover ups, false testimonies from his PR team and other slanderous lies.

These false prophets proceeded to send threatening emails to every channel of communication in the ministry over and over again. This was an evil decree against me. Maybe you have been the target of evil decrees. People have lied on you, gossiped about you, maligned you, blackmailed you, blacklisted you and blackballed you because of an evil decree. It's time to break them.

What is an Evil Decree?

An evil decree is a decree a wicked, fleshly and demonic. Evil decrees aim to cause you harm, misfortune, suffering, sorrow, distress or calamity. Although there are some similarities, an evil decree is beyond a word curse. That's why I started adding the revocation and breaking of evil decrees to my daily prayers.

Again, a decree is more than a confession. A decree is on order that carries the force of law. A decree is a command or an ordinance. A decree is similar to a curse. A curse is "prayer or invocation for harm or injury to come upon one." Goliath cursed David by His gods, but David decreed his victory.

Curses must be broken. Evil decrees must also be broken and reversed. Evil decrees, also called demonic decrees, work the enemy's plans and purposes in our life. God's decrees are congruent with His nature to give us life, in abundance, to the full, until it overflows. Evil decrees are congruent with the enemy's nature to steal kill and destroy. Evil

decrees release evil spirits to enforce the enemy's will in your life.

Evil Decrees in the Bible

We see evil decrees throughout the pages of the Bible. Pharaoh decreed all male Isralite babies be drowned in the water was over fear of losing power. Exodus 1:22, "Pharaoh charged all his people, saying, "You must cast every son that is born into the river, and you must preserve every daughter's life."

This was a mass slaughter. There were 600,000 men in Egypt, which would lead me to believe there were at least 600,00 women and hundreds of thousands of babies sacrificed to Leviathan in the Nile river during Pharaoh's reign.

The Lord showed me there's been an evil decree over some of you that's causing what you birth in your life to be devoured by the enemy. Businesses have failed because of evil decrees. Dreams have been destroyed because of evil decrees. Relationships have failed. Finances have collapsed. Health has been destroyed. Minds have been tormented.

But you can break and reverse these evil decrees, in the name of Jesus!

King Nebuchadezzar's Evil Decree

King Nebuchadnezzar issued a decree that led Shadrach, Meshach, and Abednego into the fiery furnace because people were jealous. We read the account in Daniel 3:8-18:

"Therefore at that time certain Chaldeans came near and accused the Jews. They spoke and said to King Nebuchadnezzar, "O king, live forever. You, O king, have made a decree, that every man who hears the sound of the cornet, flute, harp, sackbut, psaltery, and dulcimer, and all kinds of music should fall down and worship the golden image. And whoever does not fall down and worship should be cast into the midst of a burning fiery furnace. There are certain Jews whom you have set over the affairs of the province of Babylon: Shadrach, Meshach, and Abednego. These men, O king, have not regarded you. They do not serve your gods or worship the golden image which you have set up.

"Then Nebuchadnezzar in his rage and fury commanded Shadrach, Meshach, and Abednego be brought. Then they brought these men before the king. Nebuchadnezzar spoke and said to them, "Is it true, Shadrach, Meshach, and Abednego, that you do not serve my gods or worship the golden image which I have set up?

"Now if you are ready at the time you hear the sound of the cornet, flute, harp, sackbut, psaltery, and dulcimer, and all kinds of music to fall down and worship the image which I have made, very well. But if you do not worship, you shall be cast the same hour into the midst of a burning fiery furnace. And who is that god who can deliver you out of my hands?

"Shadrach, Meshach, and Abednego answered and said to the king, 'O Nebuchadnezzar, we do not need to give you an answer in this matter. If it be so, our God whom we serve is able to deliver us from the burning fiery furnace, and He will deliver us out of your hand, O king. But even if He does not, be it known to you, O king, that we will

not serve your gods, nor worship the golden image which you have set up."

You know the rest of the story. These three men of God ended up in a fiery furnace that was turned up to seven times the typical temperature.

Darius' Evil Decree

Even good people who do the will of God can accidentally release evil decrees through the enemy's trickery. An evil decree that led to Daniel's captivity was over jealousy and insecurity. We find this account in Daniel 6. Beginning in verse 1 through verse 15, we read:

"It pleased Darius to appoint 120 satraps to rule throughout the kingdom, with three administrators over them, one of whom was Daniel. The satraps were made accountable to them so that the king might not suffer loss. Now Daniel so distinguished himself among the administrators and the satraps by his exceptional qualities that the king planned to set him over the whole kingdom. At this, the administrators and the satraps tried to find grounds for charges

against Daniel in his conduct of government affairs, but they were unable to do so. They could find no corruption in him, because he was trustworthy and neither corrupt nor negligent. Finally these men said, "We will never find any basis for charges against this man Daniel unless it has something to do with the law of his God.

"So these administrators and satraps went as a group to the king and said: "May King Darius live forever! The royal administrators, prefects, satraps, advisers and governors have all agreed that the king should issue an edict and enforce the decree that anyone who prays to any god or human being during the next thirty days, except to you, Your Majesty, shall be thrown into the lions' den.

Now, Your Majesty, issue the decree and put it in writing so that it cannot be altered—in accordance with the law of the Medes and Persians, which cannot be repealed. "So King Darius put the decree in writing.

"Now when Daniel learned that the decree had been published, he went home to

his upstairs room where the windows opened toward Jerusalem. Three times a day he got down on his knees and prayed, giving thanks to his God, just as he had done before. Then these men went as a group and found Daniel praying and asking God for help. So they went to the king and spoke to him about his royal decree: 'Did you not publish a decree that during the next thirty days anyone who prays to any god or human being except to you, Your Majesty, would be thrown into the lions' den?'" The king answered and said, "The thing is true, according to the law of the Medes and Persians, which may not be altered. "Then they answered and said before the king, "That Daniel, who is of the sons of the captivity of Judah, does not regard you, O king, or the decree that you have signed, but makes his petition three times a day." Then the king, when he heard these words, was sorely displeased with himself and set his heart on Daniel to deliver him. And he labored until sunset to deliver him. Then these men came by agreement to the king and said to the king, "Know, O king, that it is the law of the Medes and Persians that no decree

or statute which the king establishes may be changed." You know the end of this story also. Daniel was thrown into the lion's den. The decree was irreversible. Darius was sick about it, but he was powerless to reverse the decree.

Haman's Evil Decree

Haman's evil decree was over a haughty offense. Mordecai would not bow down to Haman and Haman set out not only to destroy the man of God but his entire race. In Esther 3:8-15, Haman said to King Xerxes:

"There is a certain people dispersed among the peoples in all the provinces of your kingdom who keep themselves separate. Their customs are different from those of all other people, and they do not obey the king's laws; it is not in the king's best interest to tolerate them. If it pleases the king, let a decree be issued to destroy them, and I will give ten thousand talents of silver to the king's administrators for the royal treasury.

"The king took his signet ring from his hand and gave it to Haman, the son of Hammedatha the Agagite, the enemy of the

Jews. The king said to Haman, 'The silver has been granted to you, as have the people, so do with each as it pleases you.'

"Then the king's scribes were summoned on the thirteenth day of the first month, and a decree was written just as Haman had commanded to the king's satraps and to the governors over each province and to the officials of all peoples and to every province according to its own script, and to every people in their language. It was written in the name of King Ahasuerus and sealed with the king's signet ring. The letters were sent by mounted couriers into all the king's provinces to cause the destruction, slaughter, and annihilation of all Jews, both young and old, little children and women, in one day, the thirteenth day of the twelfth month, which is the month Adar, and even to plunder their possessions. A copy of the document, issued as law in every province, was proclaimed, calling for all people to be ready for the day.

"The couriers went out, being hastened by the king's command. At the citadel of Susa, when the decree was issued, the king and Haman sat down to drink, but

the city of Susa was in uproar."

Reversing Evil Decrees

An evil decree can be broken and reversed through a higher decree. God is not pleased with the evil decrees we release over ourselves or the evil decrees jealous, offended and otherwise wicked people release over us by inspiration of the enemy.

Take heart in Isaiah 49:24-27: "Can the prey be taken from the mighty or the captives of a tyrant be delivered? For thus says the Lord: Even the captives of the mighty shall be taken away, and the prey of the tyrant shall be delivered; for I will contend with him who contends with you, and I will save your sons.

"I will feed those who oppress you with their own flesh, and they shall be drunk with their own blood as with sweet wine. And all flesh shall know that I, the Lord, am your Savior and your Redeemer, the Mighty One of Jacob."

Please remember this: We're not wrestling against flesh and blood alone. The enemy inspires people to release evil decrees.

So, when we break and reverse evil decrees we are not seeking to harm those the enemy used against us. We're essentially sending the evil back into the enemy's camp so we can walk in God's blessing.

Every evil decree I outlined above saw a divine reversal. When we love God, He will fight for us and, as our king and judge, will turn the evil decree back on the enemy when we trust Him and take authority over the wicked words, indictments and judgments against us.

Pharaoh Reaped From His Evil Seed

Remember, Pharaoh decreed all the male babies be drowned in the water. Not only did all of Egypt lose their firstborn sons as part of the plagues Moses released at the direction of God, the Egyptian armies were drowned in water as they pursued the Israelites through the Red Sea. God made a way out of no way for the children of Israel, parting the Red Sea so they could cross on dry ground. When Pharaoh and his army tried to walk in the miracle of God, they reaped on the evil decree and sided in the sea. (See Exodus 14).

Jealous men who accused Shadrach, Meshach and Abednego Were Humiliated

Remember, an evil decree that led to Daniel's captivity was over jealousy and insecurity. Although Shadrach, Meshach, and Abednego felt some of the effects of the evil decree, the outcome was ultimately in their favor. Keep this in mind when you find yourself in a fiery furnace at the enemy's hand. We read the account in Daniel 3:21:

"Then these men were bound in their trousers, their coats, and their hats, and their other garments, and were cast into the midst of the burning fiery furnace. Therefore, because the king's commandment was urgent and the furnace exceeding hot, the flame of the fire killed those men who took up Shadrach, Meshach, and Abednego. These three men, Shadrach, Meshach, and Abednego, fell down bound into the midst of the burning fiery furnace. Then Nebuchadnezzar the king was astonished, and rose up in haste, and spoke, and said to his counselors, 'Did we not cast three men bound into the midst of the fire?'

"They answered and said to the king, 'True, O king.'

"He answered and said, 'But I see four men loose and walking in the midst of the fire, and they are unharmed. And the form of the fourth is like the Son of God!'

"Then Nebuchadnezzar came near to the mouth of the burning fiery furnace, and spoke, and said, 'Shadrach, Meshach, and Abednego, you servants of the Highest God, come out and come here!'

"Then Shadrach, Meshach, and Abednego came out of the midst of the fire. The officials, governors, and captains, and the king's counselors, being gathered together, saw these men upon whose bodies the fire had no power, nor was a hair of their head singed, neither were their coats changed, nor had the smell of fire even come upon them.

"Then Nebuchadnezzar spoke and said, 'Blessed be the God of Shadrach, Meshach, and Abednego, who has sent His angel and delivered His servants who trusted in Him. They have defied the king's word, and

yielded their bodies, that they might not serve nor worship any god, except their own God. Therefore I make a decree that every people, nation, and language which speaks anything amiss against the God of Shadrach, Meshach, and Abednego shall be cut in pieces, and their houses shall be made a dunghill, because there is no other God who can deliver in this way."

"Then the king promoted Shadrach, Meshach, and Abednego in the province of Babylon."

Men who released evil decree against Daniel devoured
Remember, an evil decree that led to Daniel's captivity was over jealousy and insecurity. We read the account in Daniel 6:17-24:

"A stone was brought and placed over the mouth of the den, and the king sealed it with his own signet ring and with the rings of his nobles, so that Daniel's situation might not be changed. Then the king returned to his palace and spent the night without eating and without any entertainment being brought to him. And he could not sleep. At the first light of dawn, the king got up and hurried to the lions' den. When he came near the den, he

called to Daniel in an anguished voice, "Daniel, servant of the living God, has your God, whom you serve continually, been able to rescue you from the lions?"

Daniel answered, 'May the king live forever! My God sent his angel, and he shut the mouths of the lions. They have not hurt me, because I was found innocent in his sight. Nor have I ever done any wrong before you, Your Majesty.' The king was overjoyed and gave orders to lift Daniel out of the den. And when Daniel was lifted from the den, no wound was found on him, because he had trusted in his God. At the king's command, the men who had falsely accused Daniel were brought in and thrown into the lions' den, along with their wives and children. And before they reached the floor of the den, the lions overpowered them and crushed all their bones.

Haman hanged on his own gallows

Remember, Haman's evil decree was over a haughty offense. Mordecai would not bow down to Haman and Haman set out not only

to destroy the man of God but his entire race. Haman thought he had the upper hand, but he hanged on the gallows made for Mordecai. Read about Mordecai's victory in Esther 7:

"So the king and Haman entered to feast and drink with Queen Esther. The king repeated to Esther what he had said on the previous day while drinking wine, 'For what are you asking, Queen Esther? It shall be granted to you. Now, what is your request? Even if it is half of the kingdom, it will be done!'

"Queen Esther replied, 'If I have found favor in your sight, O king, and if it pleases the king, at my petition, let my life be given me, and my people at my request. For we have been sold, I and my people, to be destroyed, to be slain, and to be annihilated. If only we had been sold as male and female slaves, I could have kept quiet, for that distress would not be sufficient to trouble the king.'

"Then King Ahasuerus answered and demanded of Queen Esther, 'Who is he, and

where is he, who would dare presume in his heart to do so?' "Esther said, 'This wicked Haman is the adversary and enemy!' Then Haman was seized with terror before the king and the queen. And the king arose from the banquet of wine in his wrath and went into the palace garden. But Haman remained to plead for his life from Queen Esther, for he saw that harm was determined against him by the king. Now the king returned from the palace garden back to the hall of the banquet as Haman was falling on the couch where Esther was.

"Then the king said, 'Will he also violate the queen while I am in the room?' As the shout erupted from the king's mouth, they covered the face of Haman. Then Harbona, one of the eunuchs in the king's presence, said, "The gallows, fifty cubits high, which Haman had constructed for Mordecai (who had spoken good on behalf of the king), stands at the house of Haman.' Then the king said, 'Hang him on it!' So they hanged Haman on the gallows that he had prepared for Mordecai. Then the king's wrath was pacified."

A Prayer to Break Evil Decrees

You can use this prayer as a model: I come against every decree spoken over my life, my family, my finances, my health, my relationships, and my destiny, in Jesus' name. I plead the blood of Jesus, which speaks of better things. I take authority over all the power of the enemy, including every word curse, hex, vex, spell, incantation and potion, in the name of Jesus. I decree the blessing and favor of God over every area of my life. I say I am blessed, peaceful, joyful, and prosperous. I walk in divine health. My spirit, soul and body are whole, in Jesus' name.

About Jennifer LeClaire

Jennifer LeClaire is an internationally recognized author, apostolic-prophetic voice to her generation, and conference speaker. She carries a reforming voice that inspires and challenges believers to pursue intimacy with God, cultivate their spiritual gifts and walk in the fullness of what God has called them to do. Jennifer is contending for awakening in the nations through intercession and spiritual warfare, strong apostolic preaching and practical prophetic teaching that equips the saints for the work of the ministry.

Jennifer is senior leader of Awakening House of Prayer in Fort Lauderdale, FL, founder of the Ignite Network and founder of the Awakening Blaze prayer movement.

Jennifer formerly served as the first-ever editor of *Charisma* magazine. Her work also appeared in a Charisma House book entitled *Understanding the Five-Fold Ministry* which offers a biblical study to uncover the true purpose for the fivefold ministry and *The Spiritual Warfare Bible*, which is designed to help you

use the Bible to access the power of the Holy Spirit against demonic strongholds and activity. Some of Jennifer's work is also archived in the Flower Pentecostal Heritage Museum.

Jennifer is a prolific author who has written over 25 books, including *The Heart of the Prophetic*, *A Prophet's Heart*, *Fervent Faith*, *Did the Spirit of God Say That? 27 Keys to Judging Prophecy*, *Breakthrough!*, and *Doubtless: Faith that Overcomes the World*. Some of her materials have been translated into Spanish and Korean.

Jennifer's other titles include: *The Spiritual Warrior's Guide to Defeating Jezebel*; *Developing Faith for the Working of Miracles*; *The Making of a Prophet*; *Mornings With the Holy Spirit: Listening Daily to the Still Small Voice of God* and *The Next Great Move of God: An Appeal to Heaven for Spiritual Awakening*.

Beyond her frequent appearances on the Elijah List, Jennifer writes one of *Charisma*'s most popular prophetic columns, **The Plumb Line**, and frequently contributes to *Charisma*'s

Prophetic Insight newsletter. Her media ministry includes her website; 500,000 followers on Facebook, Twitter and YouTube, Jennifer has been interviewed on numerous media outlets including USA Today, BBC, CBN, The Alan Colmes Show, Bill Martinez Live, Babbie's House, Atlanta Live and Sid Roth's It's Supernatural, as well as serving as an analyst for Rolling Thunder Productions on a *Duck Dynasty* special presentation.

Jennifer also sits on the media advisory board of the Hispanic Israel Leadership Coalition.

Jennifer is affiliated with:

Network Ekklessia International, an apostolic network founded by Dutch Sheets;

Forerunner Ministries, founded by Ken Malone;

Bill Hamon's Christian International Network;

Chuck Pierce's apostolic network

USCAL, the United States Coalition of Apostolic Leaders;

The International Society of Deliverance Ministers

Jennifer has a powerful testimony of God's power to set the captives free and claim beauty for ashes. She shares her story with women who need to understand the love and grace of God in a lost and dying world. You can also learn more about Jennifer in this broadcast on Sid Roth's *It's Supernatural.*

Other Books By Jennifer LeClaire

Angels on Assignment Again
Decoding Your Dreams
The Spiritual Warrior's Guide to Defeating Water Spirits
Releasing the Angels of Abundant Harvest
The Heart of the Prophetic
A Prophet's Heart
The Making of a Prophet
The Spiritual Warrior's Guide to Defeating Jezebel
Did the Spirit of God Say That?
Satan's Deadly Trio

Jezebel's Puppets
The Spiritual Warfare Battle Plan
Waging Prophetic Warfare
Dream Wild!
Faith Magnified
Fervent Faith
Breakthrough!
Mornings With the Holy Spirit
Evenings With the Holy Spirit
Revival Hubs Rising
The Next Great Move of God
Developing Faith for the Working of Miracles

You can download Jennifer's mobile apps by searching for "Jennifer LeClaire" in your app store and find Jennifer's podcasts on iTunes.

GET IGNITED! JOIN THE IGNITE NETWORK

I believe in prophetic ministry with every fiber of my being, but we all know the prophetic movement has seen its successes and failures. With an end times army of prophets and prophetic people rising up according to Joel

2:28 and Acts 2:17-20, it's more important than ever that we equip the saints for the work of prophetic ministry. Enter Ignite.

Ignite is a prophetic network birthed out of an encounter with the Lord that set a fire in my hearts to raise up a generation of prophets and prophetic people who flow accurately, operate in integrity, and pursue God passionately. I am laboring to cultivate a family of apostolic and prophetic voices and companies of prophets in the nations who can edify, comfort and exhort each other as we contend for pure fire in the next great move of God. My vision for Ignite covers the spiritual, educational, relational and accountability needs of five-fold ministers and intercessory prayer leaders.

You can learn more at http://www.ignitenow.org.

AWAKENING BLAZE PRAYER MOVEMENT

The Awakening Blaze mission in any city is to draw a diverse group of intercessors who have one thing in common: to contend for the Lord's will in its city, state and nation.

The vision of Awakening Blaze prayer spokes is to unite intercessors in cities across the nations of the earth to cooperate with the Spirit of God to see the second half of 2 Chronicles 7:14—"If My people, who are called by My name, will humble themselves and pray, and seek My face and turn from their wicked ways, then I will hear from heaven, and will forgive their sin and will heal their land"—come to pass.

For many years, intercessors have been repenting, praying, and seeking God for strategies. Awakening Blaze intercessors will press into see the land healed, souls saved, churches established, ministries launched, and other Spirit-driven initiatives. Blaze intercessors will help undergird other

ministries in their city, partnering with them in prayer where intercession may be lacking. Although Awakening Blaze prayer spokes are not being planted to birth churches, it is possible that churches could spring up from these intercessory prayer cells if the Lord wills.

You can find out more about this prayer movement at www.awakeningblaze.com.

You can also join the Awakening House Church Movement at awakeninghouse.com or plant a house of prayer via Awakening House of Prayer.

Printed in Great Britain
by Amazon

Unless otherwise noted, Scripture quotations are taken from the Modern English Version of the Bible.

2019: The Year of the Prophetic Decree

Published by Awakening Media
P.O. Box 30563
Fort Lauderdale, FL 33301

www.jenniferleclaire.org

2019: The Year of the Decree

A prophetic word to open the windows of heaven in your life

Jennifer LeClaire
Best-selling author of *The Making of a Prophet*